FOLD IT
AND CUT IT

FOLD IT AND CUT IT

NAOMI SHIEK

RUNNING PRESS
PHILADELPHIA · LONDON

© 2016 Quarto Inc.

Published by Running Press
An Imprint of Perseus Books, a Division of
PBG Publishing, LLC, A Subsidiary of
Hachette Book Group, Inc.

Color separation in Singapore by Pica Digital
Pte Limited

Printed in China by 1010 Printing Limited

Books published by Running Press are
available at special discounts for bulk
purchases in the United States by
corporations, institutions, and other
organizations. For more information, please
contact the Special Markets Department at
the Perseus Books Group, 2300 Chestnut
Street, Suite 200, Philadelphia, PA 19103, or
call (800) 810-4145, ext. 5000, or e-mail
special.markets@perseusbooks.com.

ISBN 978-0-7624-6104-2

Library of Congress Control Number:
2016943980

9 8 7 6 5 4 3 2 1

Digit on the right indicates the number of
this printing

Conceived, designed, and produced by
Quarto Publishing plc
The Old Brewery, 6 Blundell Street
London N7 9BH

www.quartoknows.com

Senior editor: Lily de Gatacre
Senior art editor: Emma Clayton
Designer: Joanna Bettles

Photographers: Nicki Dowey and
Phil Wilkins
Proofreader: Liz Jones
Indexer: Helen Snaith

Art director: Caroline Guest
Creative director: Moira Clinch
Publisher: Paul Carslake

Running Press Book Publishers
2300 Chestnut Street
Philadelphia, PA 19103-4371

Visit us on the web!
www.runningpress.com

CONTENTS

Papercutting is something that I stumbled into while in university. Before then, I had known papercutting only as traditional folk art, one that evoked in me memories of Victorian fairytales and gentry portraiture. On trips to my local library I found the modern evolution of papercutting, and was hooked! The work of artists such as Kara Walker and Emma van Leest mesmerized me.

What draws me to papercutting most of all is how expressive, mysterious, and fun it is to do! I never thought I'd make a career out of it, but papercutting has been infinitely rewarding and uniquely suited to my quiet nature. Give me a sunny day, Jane Austen movie adaptations on repeat, and I'm all set for a day of cutting.

Papercutting is slow, delicate work, so don't go into this thinking of a rushed, half-hour project. But if you're looking for a confidence builder, look no further: papercutting is both easy and brave. After all, cutting away delicate material with a blade to bring forth the finished design demands a certain amount of artistic courage and confidence. With a blade and paper, you can create a whole artwork that is not only beautiful in itself, but becomes more so when it interacts with its environment—the play of light and shadows, and how the papercut is used make all the difference.

Art for art's sake is lovely, but I love best papercuts that are not only beautiful but have a practical purpose. That is why I chose the projects that you will find in this book. Each can be framed up and displayed, but they can also be used as greeting cards, party decorations, holiday costumes, and more. The listed use for each project is merely a suggestion for the reader; in practice these papercuts can go as far as your imagination!

What is unique to this book is that it is filled with papercut projects of symmetrical designs, which doubles the impact in half the time! From simple mirror folds to layered papercuts, you will master the skill of papercutting with a basic blade. I hope you, too will find the same enjoyment in papercutting that I do, and through practice grow in confidence to try more and bigger templates—and even to create original designs of your own!

Naomi Shiek

There is a huge variety of paper to choose from, and in art-supply stores you'll find paper largely categorized by its intended use, such as origami, drawing, or watercolor. The important thing to know is that all of these papers can be used for papercutting; you just need to find the one that fits your project and preference.

When choosing what paper to cut, there are three variants you have to consider: weight, color, and how it slices.

The last variant is easy to find out through experimentation. If you are new to papercutting, make a trip to your local art-supply store and buy small samples of lots of different papers that appeal to you, take them home, and try cutting them. Try small shapes and big shapes, long, sweeping cuts, and tiny, intricate cuts; cut the paper flat and cut it folded. A good shape to test-cut is a leaf, as it is simple but has edges, corners, and curves—everything you're likely to encounter in papercutting projects.

You don't have to use artist quality paper to create a beautiful papercut.

You may find that you prefer to use simple printer paper or lunch-bag paper over your friend's choice of expensive acid-free watercolor paper. Your choice is personal to you, your aesthetic, and your cutting style. For instance, a paper brand that works for your friend could be a total mess for you and the way you cut, tearing and shifting under your blade instead of slicing cleanly. So make sure that you test different types and brands of paper to find the one that is best for you. As a general rule, though, if a paper has loose fibers and is "pulpy," it won't slice cleanly and won't be good for papercutting.

When thinking about paper weight (meaning thickness), consider your

papercut design. All the designs in this book are symmetrical, meaning that you will fold your paper between one and four times and will therefore be cutting through up to eight layers of paper—nine when you count the template. The heavier (or thicker) the paper is, the harder it will be for you to cut. You'll find paper-weight suggestions on each project page, but in general I advise you look for papers weighing 25–80 lb text (40–120 gsm). The thinner the paper, the more times you can fold it, and the easier it will be for you to cut intricate details.

It's important to be aware that the way paper weight is described differs between the US and Europe. In the

United States, paper weight is measured in pounds per ream. A ream is usually 500 sheets—so the heavier the ream, the thicker the paper. Printer paper is roughly 20 lb per ream, while artists' paper is roughly 100 lb per ream. In the United Kingdom and other countries, paper is measured in grams per square meter (gsm). Printer paper is roughly 80 gsm, while artists' drawing paper is roughly 150 gsm.

The paper colors you choose not only impact the finished look of your papercut project, but also how you will transfer the template to your paper (see pages 16–17). For example:
- If you mean to use a light box or window to trace your design onto your paper, you'll want to choose a light-colored paper, no heavier than 110 lb index (200 gsm).
- If you are going to use carbon paper to trace the template, the paper weight is irrelevant. Use dark carbon paper for light-colored papers and white carbon paper for dark-colored papers.
- If you want to print the template directly onto your paper, then the color just needs to be light enough for the ink to show. Most home printers will work with paper that is between 20 lb bond (75 gsm) and 60 lb cover (160 gsm).

When designing something that will be visible from both sides, make sure that the paper is colored on both sides.

For a fully personalized papercut, consider doing your design on white paper and then decorating it in your chosen colors (for example, with colored pencils, spray paint, or oil pastels).

Carbon paper

Carbon paper is a really useful material for papercutting as it will allow you to transfer designs onto your chosen paper and modify them in the process. It is available in black and white so can be used with any color paper and you will find it at office-supply and seamstress stores. Carbon paper can be used over and over, so you don't need to buy a lot of it. Just be careful—it can be a bit messy.

Carbon paper

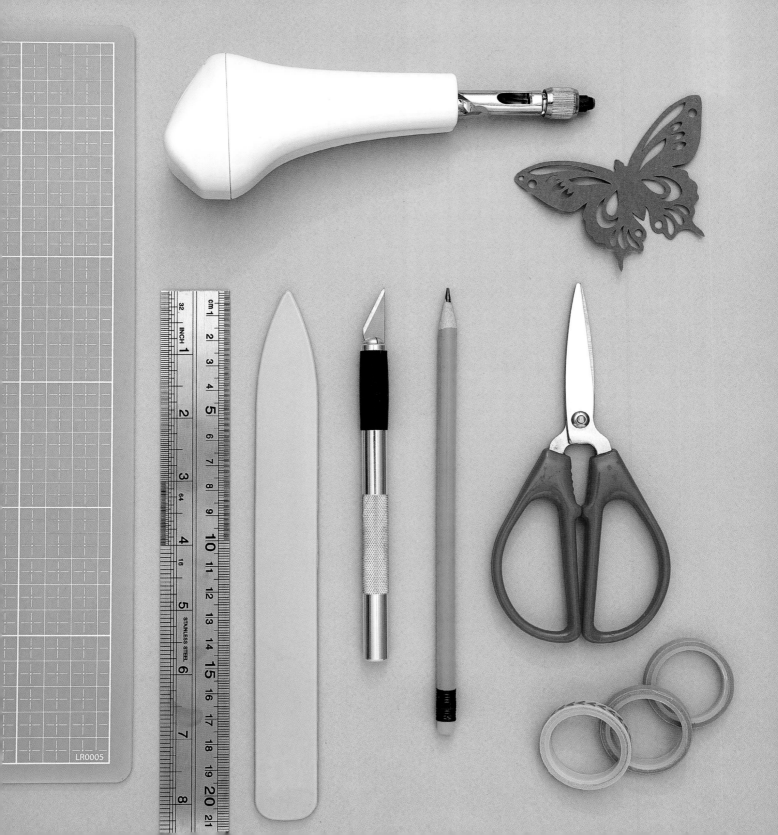

You really don't need a huge arsenal of tools to get going with papercutting, but there are definitely some tools that will make your life easier and your cutting neater.

Craft knife and blades
This is sometimes referred to as a scalpel, and is your most crucial tool. There are many models to choose from; the most popular brand—and one that's become synonymous with this type of craft knife—is X-Acto. The handles are often sold separately from the blades. Pick a handle that's light and feels comfortable in your grip. There are flexible and rotating models available, but start with a simple model first.

Standard blades usually have a 45-degree angle, but for papercutting it is ideal to have a blade with a sharper angle as it is easier to cut with. Although a 45-degree angle will work fine, if you can find blades with a 30-degree angle it will make your papercutting life easier.

I personally always buy the cheapest knife handle in the store, along with packets of 30-degree blades—my favorites are by NT Cutter. These particular blades come in strips that have to be manually broken into individual blades. If you are a beginner, I would advise buying individual blades.

Self-healing cutting mat
Widely available in craft and specialist stores, a self-healing cutting mat is the only surface you should attempt to cut on. You'll find your paper cuts more easily and cleanly on this mat, which can last for years. These come in various sizes and colors, so choose one that will fit on your work surface, and is bigger than the paper you'll be working with. The general rule of thumb is that the cutting mat should be twice the size of your project so you will have plenty of room to move and shift the paper as you cut.

Metal safeguard ruler
This is sometimes referred to as a safety ruler or a cutting ruler. It has a slightly raised edge along one side and non-slip foam on the bottom. With its non-slip bottom, the ruler won't move while you cut, which will protect your papercut and—more importantly—your fingers! Your blade will cut into plastic and wooden rulers, leaving them uneven and more likely to cause your blade to slip.

Bone folder
The name may be slightly confusing but this is actually a butter-knife-shaped tool made of plastic. The bone folder is used to etch fold lines into paper and will help you to create crisp, clean folds.

Craft screw punch
This is sometimes called a Japanese punch or a bookbinding punch and is used for creating uniform holes in paper and cardstock. Look for a model that comes with a few attachments for making holes of different sizes, between 2 and 4 mm.

Additional tools and materials
Pencil and eraser: I prefer a soft eraser pen, to easily erase small details.
Sticky tape: for attaching templates. I like to use washi tape as it is pretty and easy to remove.
Double-sided tape: for sticking layered papercuts together. You could use foam sticky dots instead for a three-dimensonal look.
Glue: either a glue stick or spray adhesive are best as they will not wet and distort the paper.
Strong task light: to keep you from straining your eyes—papercutting can be intricate work.

FOR THE ADVANCED CUTTER

Protective glasses
Although unlikely to happen, it is possible for the blade's tip to snap off into a tiny, unseen shard. I have been saved many emergency room visits due to the protection of my glasses. If you don't wear glasses, invest in a pair of protective lab goggles to keep your eyes safe from any flying debris.

Light box
A light box is not a necessity and a big window on a sunny day will do just fine (see pages 16–17). However, if you do want to buy a light box, I would recommend you choose one that uses LED lights as they stay bright and cold, so your paper won't distort with the heat—it's worth the investment. My absolute favorite light box is the LightPad by Artograph.

Silicone sleeves
These padded cushions are perfect if you are doing a lot of papercutting and will save your fingers from aching after long hours cutting! In fact, every time I cut, I wear them on the fingers I hold my knife with. I buy my silicone bandage sleeves at the pharmacy (I find them in the foot and toe section) in one long silicone sleeve that I cut to fit my fingers.

Magnifying glass with light ring
If you're getting serious about papercutting and are spending a lot of time working on very intricate designs, you might benefit from a magnifying glass. This will ease the stress on your eyesight and allow you to work well into the night.

Folds

This book is an introduction to the art of symmetrical papercuts, created by folding a piece of paper a number of times to form a complete image made of repeating shapes. In this book we will use the following five basic folds to create our symmetrical papercuts: mirror fold, quarter fold, eight fold, accordion fold, and sun fold.

HOW TO FOLD

A metal safeguard ruler and a bone folder are your best friends when folding symmetrical papercuts. Use them to score a crease line down the paper to use as a guide when folding. This will prevent the paper from creasing, splitting, or tearing when you fold it.

1 Align the metal safeguard ruler where you want the fold to be.

2 Using the bone folder, etch a line in the paper against the ruler from edge to edge.

3 Carefully fold the paper on the crease.

4 If required, use the flat of the bone folder or your fingers to smooth down the crease and flatten the fold.

MIRROR FOLD

Use this fold when you want the template to repeat itself once. Or simply put, to create a mirror image of the template. For example, the Fox Mask on pages 36–37.

1 Using the instructions at left, etch a straight line down the center of the paper.

2 Fold the paper in half widthwise. You should line up your template flush against the folded edge.

QUARTER FOLD

Choose this fold when you want the template to repeat itself four times. The image will be mirrored right to left and then again top to bottom. For example, the Shadow Box on pages 64–65.

1 Using the instructions at left, etch a straight line down the center of the paper.

2 Fold the paper in half widthwise.

3 Turn the paper 90 degrees and etch and fold it in half widthwise again.

4 You'll know you've done it right when you can count four layers of paper.

EIGHT FOLD

Use the eight fold when you want the template to repeat itself eight times. For example, the Leafy Gift Wrap on pages 32–33.

1 Using the instructions at left, etch a straight line down the center of the paper. Fold the paper in half widthwise.

2 Turn the paper 90 degrees and etch and fold it in half widthwise again.

3 Using the instructions at left, etch a straight line down the center of the paper again. This is important to ensure that the layers you have already created don't shift with this final fold. Then fold the paper in half once more. You'll know you've done it right when you can count eight layers of paper.

ACCORDION FOLD

The accordion fold is perfect when you want to create a chain of repeated patterns—like paper dolls. The Feather Crown on pages 42–43 is an example of this.

1 Measure the width of your template and mark this point from the left edge of the paper. Using the instructions at left, etch a straight line at this point.

2 Fold the left-hand edge of the paper forward using the crease you made.

3 Flip the paper over from top to bottom and fold the left-hand edge in again, using the first fold as a guide. Repeat this step until the entire paper is folded back and forth. Trim off any excess paper to end on a complete fold.

SUN FOLD

When you want the template to repeat itself eight times in a sun-burst pattern, you will use this fold. For example, the spiderweb in the Mobile project on pages 78–79. This fold works best if you start with a square piece of paper. When folding a piece of paper multiple times, it's best to etch all the fold lines first to make sure that your folded paper will be symmetrical and even in all its layers.

1 Using a metal safeguard ruler and bone folder, etch straight lines through the center of the paper from top to bottom and left to right.

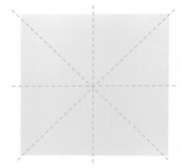

2 Also etch straight lines joining diagonally opposite corners.

3 Using the etched lines as a guide, first fold the paper in half widthwise.

4 Turn the paper 90 degrees and fold in half widthwise along the etched line.

5 Take a corner of the square and fold it to the diagonally opposite corner along the crease line you etched in Step 2.

6 You'll know you've done it right when you end up with folded paper in the shape of a triangle.

GATEWAY FOLD

There are also two fold variations included in the book: the gateway fold and the corner fold.

A gateway fold is when you use the center fold line as a guide to fold the sides of the paper in toward the center, creating a gate. For example, see the My Deer Card on pages 24–25.

1 Fold the paper in half widthwise.

2 Unfold the paper. The central crease will be your giude for completing the fold.

3 Take the right edge of the paper and fold it in toward the center, aligning the edge with the center fold line. Press down to create a sharp crease.

4 Repeat with the left edge, bringing it to meet the right edge on the center line.

CORNER FOLD

When you want to use a corner crease line as a guide for aligning and cutting your papercut template, use the corner fold. Start with a square piece of paper. For example, see the Wedding Invitation on pages 30–31.

1 Fold the paper in half widthwise.

2 Turn the paper 90 degrees so the folded edge is at the top and fold it in half widthwise again.

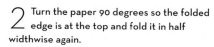

3 Take the corner of the square that has no raw edges and fold it down to the diagonally opposite corner.

4 Press the fold down with a bone folder. Align the template within the triangle shape.

5 When you unfold your papercut, you will have eight mirrored triangles.

FLATTENING YOUR WORK

Some of the projects in this book are finished by flattening the folded paper. But, as any paper crafter knows, paper doesn't like to lie flat once you've gotten your hands on it. There are three ways that I know of to flatten folded paper.

Manually

Gently run your bone folder over the crease again and again until the "peak" is flattened down.

Pressure

Put your papercut on a clean, flat surface (I use my kitchen counter). Cover it with a sheet of paper and then pile as many heavy books as you can get your hands on, on top. Leave the pile to sit for a few days; the weight of the books will flatten the paper for you.

Ironing

You do not want to dry out or burn your paper so make sure that your iron is set to its lowest heat. Put your papercut on a clean, flat surface and cover it with a tea towel or thin piece of cloth. Very gently press and move the iron from the fold line outward. The heat will flatten the paper.

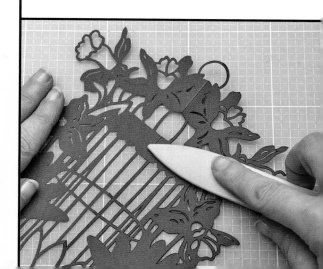

Each of the projects in this book contains full and clear instructions for creating the papercut. However, there are a few hints and tips about templates and cutting that it could help to read through before you begin.

CUT UP THIS BOOK?

If you wish, you can simply turn to the right template, cut it out, and begin! The solid parts of the templates should be left whole, the white parts cut away to reveal your design. If you don't want to cut up your book and lose the templates, you can photocopy or scan and print the template, or trace onto vellum (semi-transparent paper).

Alternatively, you can scan the QR code on page 144 and be directed to a webpage where you can access all of the templates online. From there you can reprint the templates again and again without damaging your book!

TRANSFERRING TEMPLATES

You may want to transfer the template directly onto your chosen paper. This is particularly useful if you are using a design with multiple folds, as it will reduce the number of pieces of paper you have to cut through and keep in place. To do this you can access the templates on your computer and print directly onto your chosen paper (see below) or use one of the methods described at right.

Printing onto cardstock

If you have a printer at home you can print these designs directly onto your chosen paper so that you don't have to use a template or transfer your design! Most home printers will only work with paper that is between 20 lb bond (75 gsm) and 60 lb cover (160 gsm) so bear that in mind. Remember to reverse out the template and remove the white background before you print the template so that you will cut out the colored sections and be left with your chosen color of paper. Be sure to correctly position the template on the page before you print so that it is to the right of the center line, and you can fold your paper as instructed in the project.

Using carbon paper

This is a great way of transferring templates if you are using dark-colored paper or heavy-weight cardstock. Carbon paper can be reused, so keep it safe after use.

1 Take your chosen paper, fold it as instructed in the project, and tape it to your work surface (preferably a self-healing cutting mat) using washi tape or another low-tack tape.

2 Carefully position a piece of carbon paper on top of your papercut paper, carbon side down. Choose a color of carbon paper that will be visible on your paper. Carbon paper can be a bit messy so be careful not to rub it all over your papercut paper.

3 Place your cut-out, photocopied, printed, or traced template design over both papers and tape it down.

4 Using a pen or pencil, trace over the template lines. Wherever you trace, the line will be transferred onto your papercut paper, and you can modify and customize your design as you go.

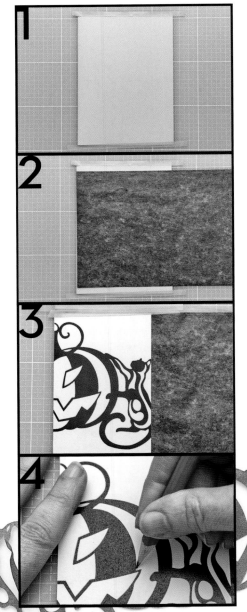

Using a window or light box

Using a light box to transfer your template straight onto your chosen paper only really works if the template is on thin paper, no more than 20 lb bond (75 gsm) or—ideally—vellum or tracing paper, and your chosen papercut paper is a pale color and weighs more than 60 lb cover (160 gsm). This is so the light will penetrate both papers and allow you to see the design below. If you're tracing using a window, you really want a sunny day! On overcast days you can bolster the light coming through by shining a light through it.

1 Take your cut-out, photocopied, printed, or traced template design and tape it to the window or light box with washi tape or another low-tack tape.

2 Position your chosen paper carefully over the template and tape it in place. You will fold the paper after you have transferred the design, so make sure the template is positioned correctly on the paper to create the symmetrical papercut.

3 The template will show through the paper and you can start tracing. It's best to use H2 pencils, as they are harder and lighter than regular #2 pencils and won't smear. An added benefit of tracing is that you can alter the image as you go and make it unique to you.

HOW TO READ A PAPERCUT

The beauty of papercutting lies in how your eyes read the design: the art of seeing the overall pattern over the mass of detail. For example, the overall shape here is a flower silhouette, but what are the "windows" cut into the paper? Your eye completes lines that aren't there and sees a bee on a flower. The windows are what is called negative space; the flower is what is called positive space.

Negative space   Positive space

My top cutting tip

The tip I got in school that stayed with me most (and saved my fingers plenty) was to NOT press down hard as I cut. If the paper feels too thick and the blade doesn't go through on the first go, go over the cut twice, three times. Yes, it takes longer, but it saves your fingers from blisters and wayward blades.

CUTTING TIPS

Cutting symmetrical papercuts has its own unique challenges, regardless of the design. The more you fold the paper, the thicker it becomes and the harder it is for a blade to cut through. If the paper is hard to cut, it is more likely that the folded layers will shift as you cut, ruining the symmetrical effect. These tips will help you to cut comfortably, cut neatly, and—most importantly—cut safely.

• Before you begin, tape the paper to the cutting mat. You can tape the folded layers together using double-sided tape as well to prevent the layers shifting as you work.

• Hold the paper as you cut, but keep your fingers away from the blade! Hold your palm flat on the paper and cut away from you.

• Use a comfortable knife handle. Slip a cushioned pencil grip on it if your fingers feel bruised, or use a silicone sleeve (see page 11) on your fingers.

• For sharp, clean lines, use sharp-angle blades (I use 30-degree blades). The sharper the angle, the thinner the tip is that drags along the paper, so the cut is cleaner, especially when cutting curves.

• Always cut the smallest shapes first, and those closest to the fold line. The larger the cut and the farther from the fold, the more the integrity of the paper is affected.

• Don't try to cut large or complex shapes in one go without lifting the blade. Cut one side of a shape then return to the starting point to cut the other side. It will be easier and cleaner if you always cut in the direction most natural to you instead of fighting yourself and cutting "against the grain."

• The templates are guidelines only—don't worry about accurately cutting shapes that feel too small or too big to you. Let your hand move in the direction that feels right. You'll find the experience is improved for it, and the papercut lovelier.

PROJECTS

KISSING SQUIRRELS CARD

This beautiful papercut card is perfect for a Valentine or special loved one. It features the simple mirror fold and the design is cut out from the edge of the paper, farthest from the fold.

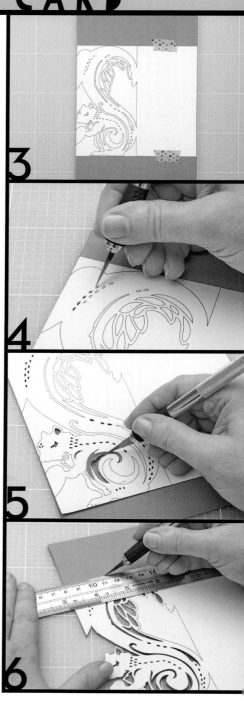

Tool kit
• Bone folder
• Metal safeguard ruler
• Self-healing cutting mat
• Craft knife and blades

Materials
• Printer paper
• Thin cardstock in two contrasting colors
• Sticky tape
• Double-sided tape

Choosing materials
When selecting your cardstock for this project, remember that the thickness will double when folded. The thicker the paper, the harder it will be to cut through. I'd recommend a maximum of 80 lb text (120 gsm).

1 Cut out template 1 on page 89. To use the template more than once, print, copy, or transfer the template using one of the methods on page 16. The printed template will be cut and discarded, and the finished papercut will have no visible guidelines on either side.

2 Take a piece of thin cardstock for the papercut part of the card. Using a bone folder and metal ruler, fold the cardstock in half widthwise. Use the bone folder to apply even pressure when folding to create a clean crease.

3 Place the printed template on the cardstock with the straight edge flush against the folded edge and the squirrel's nose against the open edge. Tape the template to the cardstock so it won't move as you work—I like to use colorful washi tape.

4 Using a craft knife on a cutting mat, start by carefully cutting out all of the tiny leaf shapes, before moving to the squirrel's ear and eye. When you're cutting, don't press down hard—you risk breaking the blade or losing control of the knife. It is better to make two or three passes with the blade over the same area. Trust me, the extra seconds taken are far preferable to a cut finger or slashed template!

5 Cut the rest of the details on the fur, from the body up to the tail. When you're cutting the longer and circular shapes, don't try to cut them in one pass. Lift the blade and make multiple cuts from different angles for better control.

6 Cut the outline of the squirrel. To cut the straight lines of the bottom of the squirrel and the card outline, use a non-slip metal ruler with a finger guard.

Template is on page 89

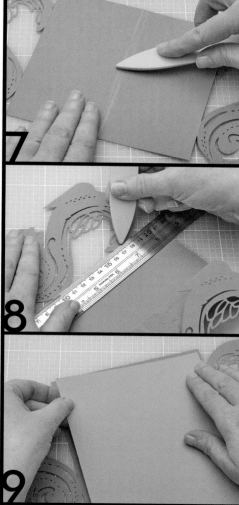

7 Unfold the card and use the bone folder to smooth down the crease line.

8 Carefully fold each squirrel over toward the center of the card. To do this, place the metal ruler along the join between the card and squirrel section and use the bone folder to etch a sharp crease line—this will guide your fold. As you fold, apply even pressure with the bone folder to smooth down the crease and create a clean fold.

9 Take your contrasting color of cardstock and use a craft knife and metal rule on a cutting mat to cut a square very slightly smaller than the central square of the card. Attach this insert to the inside of your card using small strips of double-sided tape. This will be where you write your love note.

MY DEER CARD

This beautiful card is lovely for any occasion, but it is for the patient cutter! Although it's not a complex design, cutting all those leaves can be time-consuming—but the effect is well worth the effort.

Tool kit
- Bone folder
- Metal safeguard ruler
- Self-healing cutting mat
- Craft knife and blades

Materials
- Medium-weight cardstock
- Colored paper for insert
- Sticky tape
- Double-sided tape

Choosing materials
You want your card to stand up when it is finished so it's best to use a medium-weight cardstock for the main part of the card—I would recommend 60 lb cover (160 gsm). Try using a contrasting color paper for the insert.

1 Cut out template 2 on page 91. To use the template more than once, print, copy, or transfer the template using one of the methods on page 16.

2 Cut a piece of medium-weight cardstock the same height as the template and four times the width. Using a bone folder and metal ruler, fold the cardstock in half widthwise. Unfold.

3 Take the left-hand edge and, using the metal ruler and bone folder, fold it to meet the central crease.

4 Flip the paper over so that the folded edge is now on the right and folds under. Place the template on the cardstock flush against the folded edge. Tape the template to the cardstock so it won't move as you work.

5 Using a craft knife on a cutting mat, first carefully cut out all the small leaf shapes. Be patient.

6 Next cut out the shape of the deer and his antlers. Take your time and be careful not to cut through the thin lines of the antlers.

Template is on page 91

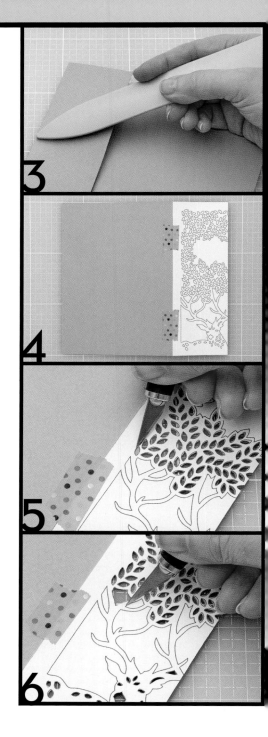

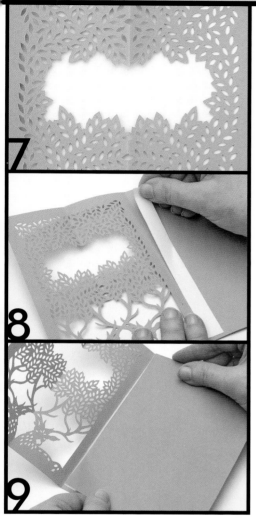

7 Finally, cut out the void in the center
of the leaves. You don't have to try
and cut large shapes all in one go. Lift the
blade every now and then and make
multiple smaller cuts. Remove the
template carefully and unfold the card.

8 Open up the card so that you are
looking at the inside of the greeting
card. Place a strip of double-sided tape
just to right of the central crease line.
This is how you will fix your colored
insert paper.

9 Take a piece of paper in a contrasting
color and cut it to the same size as
your piece of cardstock. Fold it in half
widthwise and carefully stick to the
double-sided tape inside the card, aligning
the folded edge with the central crease.

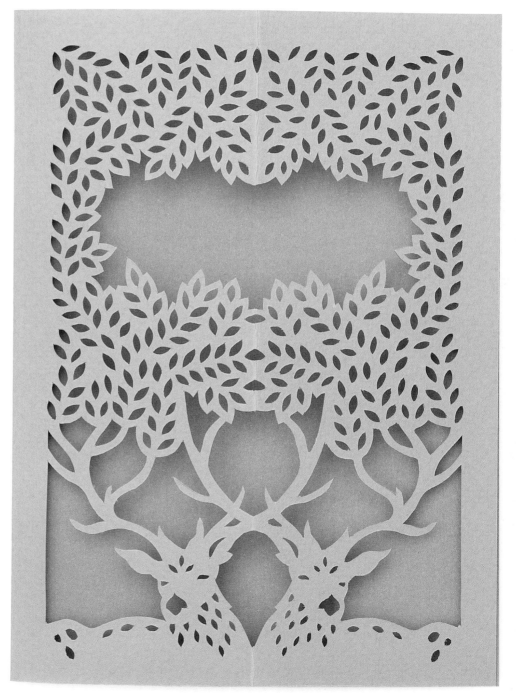

These intricate leaves can be used with the gift wrap on pages 32–33 and the ribbon on pages 40–41 to form part of a gift wrap set. Used on their own they'll be a lovely addition to any thoughtful gift.

Tool kit
- Bone folder
- Metal safeguard ruler
- Self-healing cutting mat
- Craft knife and blades
- Craft screw punch

Materials
- Heavy-weight cardstock in three colors
- Printer paper (optional)
- Sticky tape (optional)
- Double-sided tape
- Twine or ribbon

Choosing materials
The layers of this delicate gift tag need to be made on heavy-weight cardstock so that the tag keeps its shape and structure—about 110 lb cover (270 gsm). Heavy-weight cardstock is more difficult to cut through so it is not a good idea to cut the templates out from the back of the book as that will add another thick layer to cut through. It is better to use printer paper or, better yet, transfer the template directly onto your cardstock.

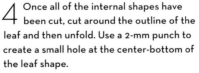

Template is on page 97

1 Turn to template 6 on page 97. Use one of the methods on page 16 to transfer the three parts of the template to your chosen cardstock. Alternatively, photocopy the template or access using the QR code and print onto regular printer paper, and tape to the cardstock. Whichever method you use, position the templates right of center on the cardstock and use a different color for each template.

2 Using a bone folder and metal ruler, fold the cardstock so that the center of the leaf aligns with the folded edge.

3 Using a craft knife on a cutting mat, start by carefully cutting out all of the internal shapes on the medium-sized leaf. To prevent the paper from shifting as you work, tape the two layers together at the open edge using double-sided tape. The tape will be cut off with the rest of the excess cardstock, so you'll be able to unfold the papercut later. Start by cutting the shapes nearest to the folded edge and then move outward.

4 Once all of the internal shapes have been cut, cut around the outline of the leaf and then unfold. Use a 2-mm punch to create a small hole at the center-bottom of the leaf shape.

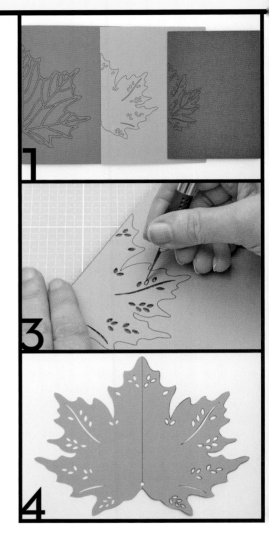

5

6

5 Repeat Steps 3–4 with the other two leaves.

6 Layer your leaf shapes with the largest at the back and the smallest at the front. Align the holes you've made at the bottom of each leaf. Cut a length of twine or ribbon and thread it through the three holes to join the three leaves, and knot to secure.

This unique card is made out of three different-colored layers and could suit any occasion. But with plenty of room for text inside and lots of options for adding further embellishments, this makes the ultimate papercut wedding invitation.

Tool kit
- Bone folder
- Metal safeguard ruler
- Self-healing cutting mat
- Craft knife and blades
- Tweezers (optional)

Materials
- Paper in three colors
- Sticky tape
- Double-sided tape
- Glue (spray adhesive or glue stick)
- Faux rhinestones (optional)

Choosing materials
Your card will be made up of three layers of paper, which will give it some bulk, so you needn't use heavy- or even medium-weight cardstock to begin with. I would recommend 20 lb (80 gsm).

Template is on page 101

1 Cut out template 13 on page 101. To use the template more than once, print, copy, or transfer the template using one of the methods on page 16.

2 Choose the paper for the papercut part of your card and, using a craft knife and metal ruler on a cutting mat, cut an 8¼-inch (21-cm) square.

3 Fold the paper in half and then in half again to form quarters. Use the bone folder to make the creases as smooth and flat as possible. If the paper is colored on only one side, make sure that you fold it with the colored side inside.

4 Tape the triangular template to the paper with two edges flush against the two outside edges of the paper—not along the folded edge.

5 Using a craft knife and metal ruler on a cutting mat, first cut along all the border lines of the template.

6 Then cut out the internal shapes, working from the border inward. Remove the template and unfold the paper.

7 Choose a piece of paper in a contrasting color to be the backing to your papercut. Take a piece larger than 8¼ inches (21 cm) square and, using spray adhesive or a glue stick, stick to the back of your papercut. Once the glue is dry, trim the backing paper exactly to size, using a craft knife and a metal ruler on a cutting mat.

8 With the papercut part on the outside, fold the square in half from top to bottom, using a bone folder to make a sharp crease, and unfold. Now fold the left edge to the right edge, using a bone folder to make a sharp crease, and unfold. Lay the papercut face down.

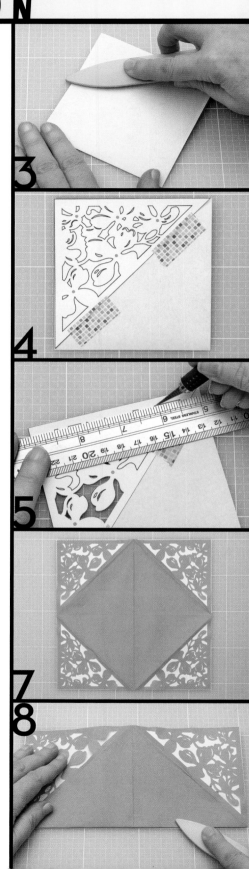

Try template 14 or 15 on page 101 for a slightly different design.

9 Take one corner and, using the crease lines you have already made as a guide, fold the corner down so the tip meets the center point of the square. Use a bone folder to create sharp, crisp creases.

10 Repeat with the other three corners until you have a smaller square with the papercut corners facing up.

11 Take your third colored paper and, using a craft knife and metal ruler on a cutting mat, cut a 5$^1/_2$-inch (14-cm) square for your text layer. Using spray adhesive or a glue stick, attach this paper to the inside of your papercut square.

12 Use a pair of tweezers to carefully glue some rhinestones to your papercut for a bit of extra oomph.

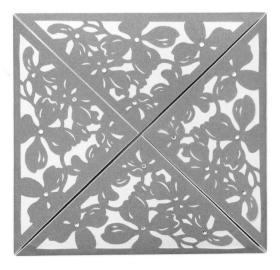

I bet you never thought you could create your own papercut gift wrap—but you can! This is guaranteed to wow your friends and it's fairly simple to create. You could even team it with the gift tag on pages 26–27 and the ribbon on pages 40–41 for an impressive set.

Tool kit
- Bone folder
- Metal safeguard ruler
- Pencil
- Self-healing cutting mat
- Craft knife and blades

Materials
- Printer paper
- Two sheets of wrapping paper in contrasting colors
- Carbon paper
- Sticky tape

Choosing materials
You'll be cutting through eight layers of paper at a time so a nice, thin wrapping paper of about 20 lb bond (75 gsm) would be ideal. The thinner the paper, the easier it will be to cut. Think about the color of the papers you choose, as one will show through the other. Go for a bold contrast or stick to more similar colors for a subtle design.

Template is on page 95

1 Cut out template 5 on page 95. To use the template more than once, print or copy the template using one of the methods on page 16. You will be transferring the design onto your chosen paper.

2 Take the wrapping paper that will feature the papercut design and fold it in half lengthwise three times. If the wrapping paper is colored on only one side, make sure that you fold it with the colored side inside. The sheets of wrapping paper used in this example are 18 x 25½ inches (45 x 65 cm) in size.

3 You will be cutting through multiple layers here, and adding another layer in the form of a template (even just printer paper) will make cutting more difficult, so it's best to transfer the template directly to the paper. Tape the folded wrapping paper to the cutting mat so the layers don't shift, and place a piece of carbon paper on top. Align the template on top of the carbon paper and tape this firmly onto the mat so it doesn't move.

4 Carefully trace over the template with a pencil. This will transfer the design onto the top layer of wrapping paper. Remove the tape and discard the template and carbon paper.

5 Using a craft knife on a cutting mat, cut the leaves one by one. If you're left-handed, cut from right to left. If you're right-handed, cut from left to right. This will stop your hand from dragging and ripping the thin wrapping paper.

6 Unfold the wrapping paper to reveal your design. Layer the papercut wrapping paper over a plain wrapping paper in a contrasting color to make your gift wrapping really interesting.

SWAN NECKLACE

You really can create anything out of paper—including jewelry. This statement necklace is a fun project and a great way to try out layered papercuts.

Tool kit
• Bone folder
• Metal safeguard ruler
• Self-healing cutting mat
• Craft knife and blades
• Craft screw punch or hole punch

Materials
• Printer paper (optional)
• Heavy-weight cardstock
• Sticky tape (optional)
• Double-sided tape
• Foam sticky dots (optional)
• Twine or ribbon

Choosing materials
Choose cardstocks in colors that will stand out against each other. For example: pink and red, or black and white. This is a great opportunity to try papers with colorful patterns or contrasting tones. Go wild.

Template is on page 109

1 Turn to template 22 on page 109. Use one of the methods on page 16 to transfer both parts of the template to your chosen cardstock. This way you will not have any extra layers or templates to contend with. Alternatively, photocopy the template or access using the QR code and print onto regular printer paper, and tape to the cardstock. Whichever method you use, position the templates right of center on the cardstock and choose a different color for each template.

2 Take the cardstock with the swan on and fold it in half lengthwise with the design facing up. The beak of the swan should align exactly along the center crease. To cleanly fold the cardstock, first lay the metal ruler in the correct place and use the bone folder to etch a sharp crease line—this will guide your fold. As you fold, apply even pressure with the bone folder to smooth down the crease and create a clean fold.

3 Using a craft knife and metal ruler on a cutting mat, start by cutting the tiny shapes within the swan first and moving onto the larger shapes.

4 Using a craft screw punch or an office hole punch, punch a hole through both layers of paper at the top of the swan's wing. You will use this later to assemble the necklace.

5 Carefully cut around the outline of the swan, and unfold.

6 Take the cardstock with the wing template on and, using a metal ruler and bone folder, fold the cardstock in half.

7 Cut the internal shapes of the wing, beginning with the tiny feathers and moving onto the larger ones. To prevent the paper from shifting as you work, you may want to tape the two layers together at the

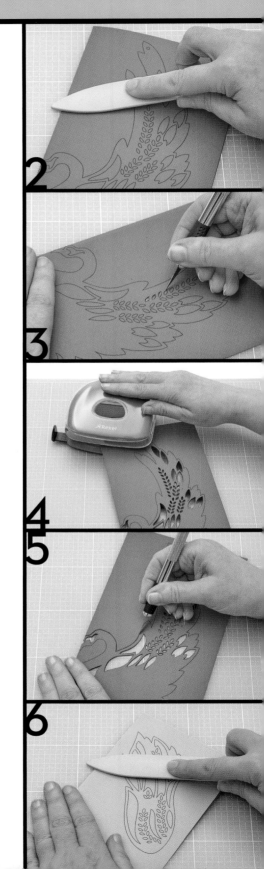

7

8

9

open edge using double-sided tape. The tape will be cut off with the rest of the excess cardstock. Cut around the outline of the wing—you will be left with two separate wings.

8 Using strips of double-sided tape, attach the wings to the swan, aligning the bottom edges. To give your necklace a more three-dimensional look, attach the wings with foam sticky dots.

9 Cut two lengths of twine or ribbon, thread them through the holes at the top of the back wings, and tie in knots to secure. Your statement necklace is ready to wear.

This simple design is a great introduction to the art of symmetrical papercutting. It uses only one fold and will familiarize you with common shapes and basic principles that you'll encounter in this book. And you'll get a fun costume to boot!

Tool kit
- Bone folder
- Metal safeguard ruler
- Self-healing cutting mat
- Craft knife and blades

Materials
- Printer paper (optional)
- Medium-weight cardstock
- Sticky tape
- Ribbon

Choosing materials
I would recommend you use a medium-weight cardstock of approximately 80 lb text–60 lb cover (120–160 gsm) for this project. The mask needs to be flexible enough to slightly curve around your head but strong enough to withstand a bit of stress, without tearing.

Template is on page 111

1 Turn to template 23 on page 111. Use one of the methods on page 16 to transfer the template to your chosen cardstock. This way you will not have any extra layers or templates to contend with. Alternatively, photocopy the template or access using the QR code and print onto regular printer paper, and tape to the cardstock. Whichever method you use, position the templates right of center on the cardstock.

2 Fold the cardstock in half lengthwise with the design facing up. The edge of the template should align exactly along the center crease. To cleanly fold the cardstock, first lay the metal ruler in the correct place and use the bone folder to etch a sharp crease line—this will guide your fold. As you fold, apply even pressure with the bone folder to smooth down the crease and create a clean fold.

3 Using a craft knife and metal ruler on a cutting mat, start by cutting the tiny shapes first, beginning with those closest to the folded edge and working outward. Starting with the small shapes helps to ensure the paper's integrity and makes it easier to handle. Otherwise the paper could move and tear as you work.

4 Very carefully cut the shapes that fall on the fold itself.

5 Move onto the larger leaf-like shapes. It is best to continue working from the folded edge outward.

6 The final internal shapes to cut are the eye and the inside ear. Remember to start with the smallest shapes and move onto the larger shapes. The more you cut, the more delicate the paper becomes.

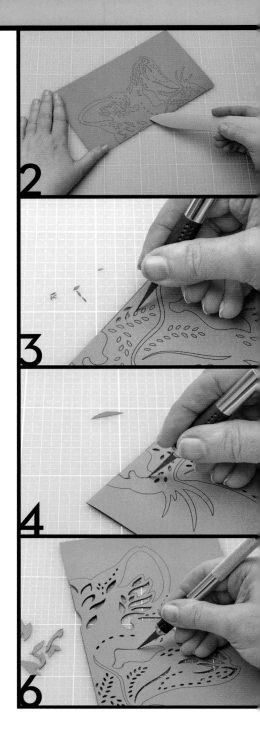

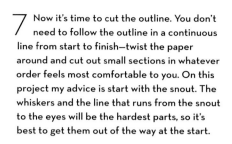

7 Now it's time to cut the outline. You don't need to follow the outline in a continuous line from start to finish—twist the paper around and cut out small sections in whatever order feels most comfortable to you. On this project my advice is start with the snout. The whiskers and the line that runs from the snout to the eyes will be the hardest parts, so it's best to get them out of the way at the start.

8 Unfold your mask to reveal the pattern. Use the bone folder to smooth down the central crease.

9 Cut two lengths of ribbon and tie them to cutouts at either side of the fox's face. Where you add the ribbon is up to you and will determine the placement of the mask on your face. The fox's eye sockets should align with your eyes. The fox's snout will be pushed forward by your nose and will slightly stick out to accommodate your features, so the mask will fit both adults and children.

LEAFY RIBBON

This project is a lovely way to add a personal touch to a beautifully wrapped gift. It's wonderful on its own, or you could combine it with the gift tag on pages 26–27 and the gift wrap on pages 32–33 for a complete set.

Tool kit
- Bone folder
- Metal safeguard ruler
- Pencil
- Self-healing cutting mat
- Craft knife and blades

Materials
- Printer paper
- Paper
- Carbon paper
- Sticky tape

Choosing materials
You want to be able to wrap your papercut ribbon easily around a gift, just as you would a fabric ribbon, so you don't want to use thick cardstock here. I would recommend 28 lb bond (105 gsm) paper instead. You may also be cutting through multiple layers, so a thinner paper will make your life easier.

1 Turn to template 7 on page 97. You may need to resize this template to suit your specific needs. For example, if you need an 18-inch (45-cm) length of ribbon, resize the template to 6 inches (15 cm) long. Use the QR code to access the templates on your computer, resize the template to the desired size, and print onto printer paper. Alternatively, you can resize the templates using a photocopier.

2 Take your chosen paper and, using a bone folder and metal ruler, accordion fold the paper (see page 13) to fit your template. In this example, my template is 6 inches (15 cm) long, so I will accordion fold my 18-inch (45-cm) strip of paper every 6 inches (15 cm). Remember that the more layers of paper you have, the harder it will be to cut through.

3 You will be cutting through multiple layers here, and adding another layer in the form of a template (even just printer paper) will make cutting more difficult, so it's best to transfer the template directly to the paper with carbon paper. Tape the accordion-folded paper to the cutting mat so the layers don't shift and place a piece of carbon paper on top. Align the template on top of the carbon paper and tape this firmly onto the mat so it doesn't move.

4 Carefully trace over the template with a pencil. This will transfer the design onto the top layer of your folded paper. Remove the tape and discard the template and carbon paper.

5 Using a craft knife and metal ruler on a cutting mat, begin by cutting all of the small shapes—the lines and the leaves—in the center of the design.

Template is on page 97

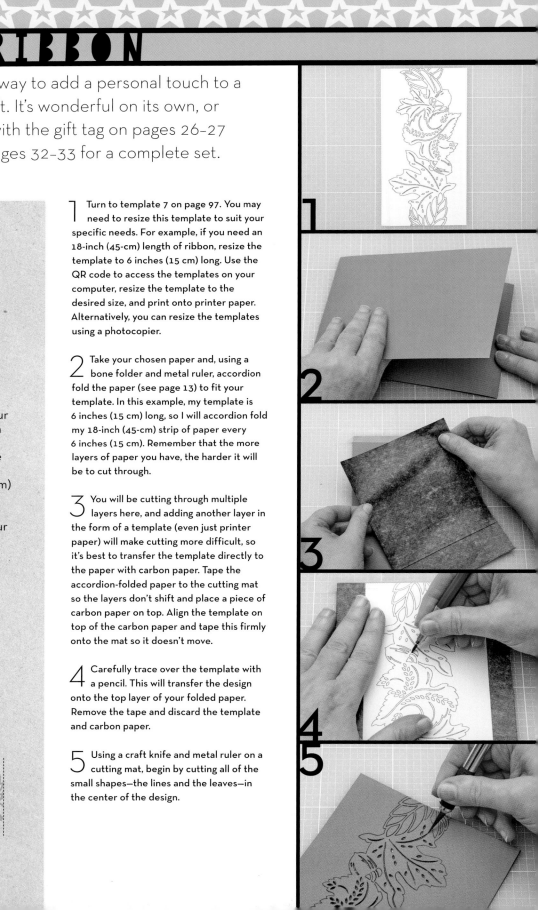

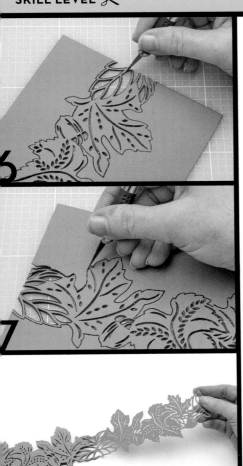

6 Cut the details on the acorns and the larger leaves toward the ends of the template. Take particular care here—be careful not to cut through the connecting paper in the folds.

7 Now focus on cutting the outline of the template.

8 Unfold the papercut ribbon. Carefully wrap it around your gift, making sure to put the side you drew on face down in case of any remaining pencil marks. Add more sections as needed and tape together in place for instant gift impact.

FEATHER CROWN

This project was created specifically for kings and queens! An accordion fold turns this simple design into a stunner for kids and adults alike.

Tool kit
- Tape measure
- Bone folder
- Metal safeguard ruler
- Self-healing cutting mat
- Craft knife and blades

Materials
- Paper in two contrasting colors
- Sticky tape

Choosing materials
You can make this project from any regular printer or craft paper—just glue or tape a few pieces together (approximately two for a child, three for an adult) to get to the right length. Stick to a maximum weight of 20 lb bond (75 gsm) as there are quite a few folds in this piece.

Template is on page 105

1 Turn to template 18 on page 105. Use one of the methods on page 16 to transfer the template to your chosen paper. This way you will not have any extra layers or templates to contend with. Alternatively, photocopy the template or access using the QR code and print onto regular printer paper, and tape to the paper. Whichever method you use, position the template at the edge of the paper.

2 To work out how many times you need to fold your paper, first measure the circumference of your head and divide this by the width of the template. This will tell you how much paper you need, how many repeats of the pattern, and how many times you need to fold your paper.

3 Accordion fold the paper making sure your template stays on top (see page 13). Use a bone folder to ensure crisp folds.

4 Using a craft knife on a cutting mat, start by cutting the small leaves along the border at the bottom of the crown, and the two stars.

5 Start cutting the feather from the center shape and work your way outward until the feather is complete.

6 Cut the outline of the crown, being careful that the layers do not shift as you cut. Make sure not to cut through the accordion fold or else the repeat will be broken. Unfold the crown to reveal the pattern.

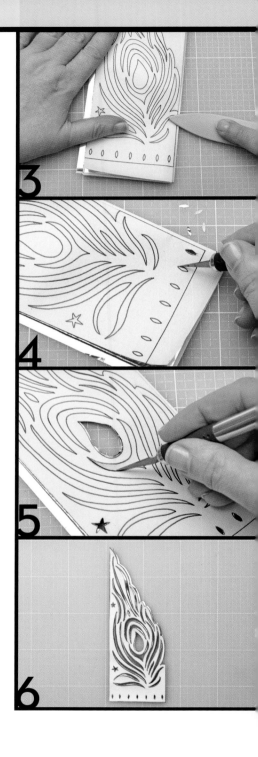

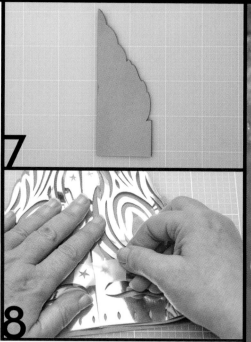

7 You could leave your crown as it is, or,
to make it fit for royalty, continue to
create another, contrasting, layer. Print
another crown template, or reuse the
original and repeat Steps 1–3 and then
jump to Step 6, so you are only cutting
around the outline of the crown.

8 Line up the two layers and use glue
or double-sided tape to attach them
together. Tape the long strip into a
circular shape to complete the crown.

This gift card reveals a secret message in its center. It makes a great birthday card for any little princess.

Tool kit
- Bone folder
- Metal safeguard ruler
- Self-healing cutting mat
- Craft knife and blades

Materials
- Light- to medium-weight cardstock in two contrasting colors
- Sticky tape
- Glue (spray adhesive or glue stick)

Choosing materials
To make your life easier, why not use a lighter-weight cardstock for the papercut portion of the card, which involves far more intricate cutting. You can give the card some structure with a heavier-weight cardstock for the background that doesn't need as much cutting—or any folding. Make sure that the color you choose for the background is light enough that your message will show up.

1 Cut out template 4 on page 93. To use the template more than once, print, copy, or transfer the template using one of the methods on page 16.

2 Take a piece of the cardstock for the papercut portion of your card—it should be at least as tall and twice as wide as the template. Using a metal ruler and bone folder, fold the cardstock in half widthwise. Scoring the line first will help you to create a sharp crease.

3 Place the printed template on the cardstock with the center of the design flush against the folded edge. Tape the template in place. From here we have removed the template for clarity.

4 Using a craft knife on a cutting mat, start by cutting the brickwork on the castle and the leaves. Remember that the shapes are only a guideline—don't worry about accurately tracing any shapes that feel too tight or small. Let your hand move in the way that feels most natural to you. This way you'll find the experience is more fun and the papercut turns out better. And once the template is removed and your design is left, you won't remember any artistic licenses you took.

5 Cut the windows and the slightly larger decorative details on the castle. Then cut around the outline.

6 Cut out the details in the gate. Then, very carefully cut the yellow curved arch and use a metal ruler to help you cut the bottom line of the gate. Do not cut the dashed line along the side of the gate.

Template is on page 93

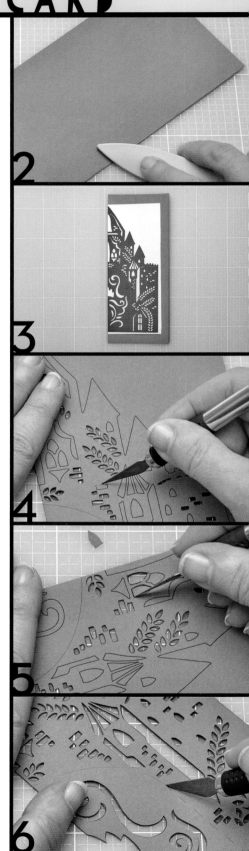

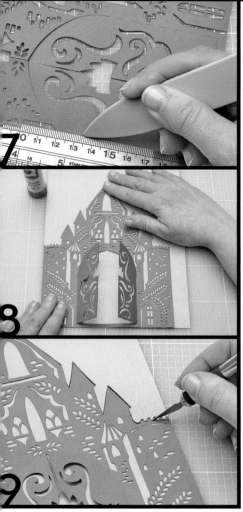

7 Remove the template and unfold the card. You'll notice that the gate is still closed. Using the metal ruler on a cutting mat, cut down the center line to open the gate. Fold the doors open. It will help to ease the fold if you first etch the fold lines using a bone folder and metal ruler.

8 Take your second colored paper, which will form the backing of the card, where your secret message will be written. Glue the papercut layer on top of the backing layer.

9 Cut out the outline of the castle. Remember to use a ruler on the straight lines and turn the card as you cut to help you navigate the twists and turns.

Projects

Families come in all shapes and sizes, and you can add as many leaves to this papercut tree as you need to.

Tool kit
- Bone folder
- Metal safeguard ruler
- Self-healing cutting mat
- Craft knife and blades

Materials
- Medium-weight cardstock in two colors
- Glue, double-sided tape, or foam sticky dots

Choosing materials
I would recommend using cardstock of approximately 65 lb cover (176 gsm) for this project. There is only one fold and not many tiny bits to cut out, and this will give your family tree a nice structure.

1   Cut out template 24 on page 113. To use the template more than once, print, copy, or transfer the template using one of the methods on page 16.

2   Take a piece of the cardstock for the tree—it should be at least as tall and twice as wide as the template. Using a metal ruler and bone folder, fold the cardstock in half widthwise. Scoring the line first will help you to create a sharp crease.

3   Place the printed template on the cardstock with the trunk flush against the folded edge. Tape the template in place. From here we have removed the template for clarity.

4   Using a craft knife on a cutting mat, start by cutting the internal details on the animals: the squirrel and the cat in the tree, and the deer in the grass.

5   Cut the branches of the tree, starting with those farthest from the folded edge and working inward. When you get to the beehive on the fold line, be careful not to shift the paper. Hold your palm flat against the paper to keep it in place, and cut away from you. If you're left-handed, move the blade from right to left. If you're right-handed, turn the paper upside down and cut from left to right.

Template is on page 113

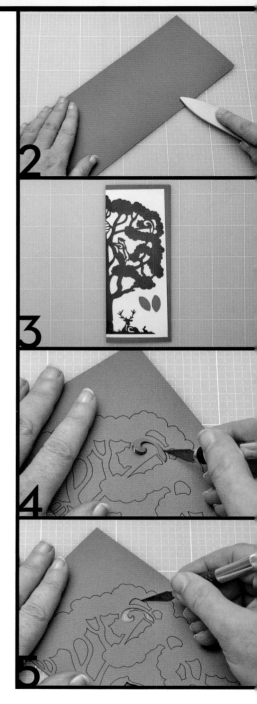

6 Cut all along the outline, starting at the grass. Be careful around the deer's antlers and the little bunny rabbit. Remove the template and unfold the tree. Use a bone folder to flatten the central crease.

7 Take your second colored cardstock and fold the paper in half using a bone folder. Attach the leaf templates with tape. How many leaves do you need? That's entirely up to you. If your cardstock isn't too thick, you could fold it in half again to create four leaves from each template. Cut out the leaves.

8 Use glue, double-sided tape, or foam sticky dots to attach the leaves to your tree wherever you like. Write on the names of your family members.

This simple mirror-fold papercut requires some delicate cutting. Be patient and you will create a beautiful artwork fit for framing.

Tool kit
• Bone folder
• Metal safeguard ruler
• Self-healing cutting mat
• Craft knife and blades

Materials
• Thin cardstock in two colors
• Sticky tape
• Spray adhesive

Choosing materials
Cardstock of approximately 80 lb text (120 gsm) is about right for this project. You could use heavier-weight cardstock for the background, as this doesn't involve folding and cutting. Think about the colors for the papercut and the background, and make sure they go well together.

Template is on page 103

1 Cut out template 16 on page 103. To use the template more than once, print, copy, or transfer the template using one of the methods on page 16.

2 Take a piece of the cardstock you have chosen for the main papercut at least as tall and twice as wide as the template. Using a metal ruler and bone folder, fold the cardstock in half widthwise. Scoring the line first will help you to create a sharp crease.

3 Place the printed template on the cardstock with the center of the birdcage flush against the folded edge. Tape the template in place. From here we have removed the template for clarity.

4 Using a craft knife on a cutting mat, cut the tiny details on the sunflower and the daffodil. You could omit these very delicate cuts for a slightly easier, but still beautiful, project.

5 Cut the rest of the daffodil and move onto the waterlily at the bottom of the design. When cutting the waterlily, start at the farthest point from the folded edge and work your way inward.

6 Start at the top of the birdcage and work your way down. First slowly cut all of the vertical lines, working from right to left, and only then start cutting the short horizontal lines at the top and bottom of the bars. This will help prevent the paper from shifting.

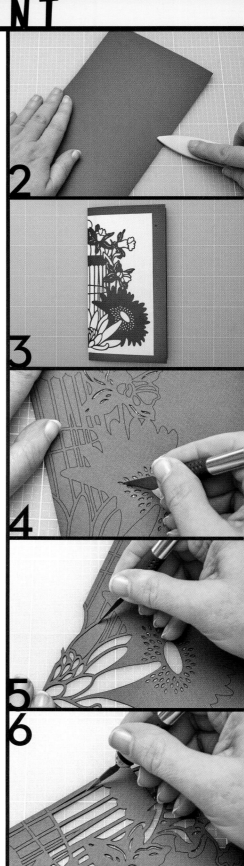

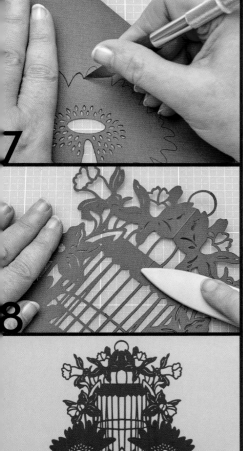

7 Carefully cut around the outline of the template.

8 Remove the template and unfold the papercut. Use a bone folder to flatten the central crease.

9 Use spray adhesive to attach the papercut to the background. If necessary, trim the background cardstock to size, and then frame.

FAIRY RING CARD

This whimsical card is perfect for a birthday or a party invitation, with plenty of space for a personalized message.

Tool kit
- Bone folder
- Metal safeguard ruler
- Self-healing cutting mat
- Craft knife and blades
- Craft screw punch (optional)

Materials
- Medium-weight cardstock
- Sticky tape

Choosing materials
Choose cardstock of roughly 60 lb cover (160 gsm) so that it is easy for you to cut through two layers but the little details won't be at risk of tearing off.

Template is on page 91

1 Cut out template 3 on page 91. To use the template more than once, print, copy, or transfer the template using one of the methods on page 16.

2 Take a piece of the cardstock you have chosen for the main papercut at least as tall and twice as wide as the template. Using a metal ruler and bone folder, fold the cardstock in half widthwise. Scoring the line first will help you to create a sharp crease.

3 Place the printed template on the cardstock with the center of the mushroom flush against the folded edge. Tape the template in place. From here we have removed the template for clarity.

4 Using a craft knife on a cutting mat, cut the small details inside the cap of the mushroom. Start with those farthest away from the fold and work inward. You can use a screw punch instead of the blade for these details if you like.

5 Cut the ribbon-like details, starting with those farthest from the folded edge and working inward.

6 Cut the outline of the card. Start with the grass and cut from the base up. If you cut into the base, the paper may drag and the little grass blades could tear. Use a metal ruler to help you cut the straight side and bottom of the card.

7 Remove the template and unfold the papercut. Use a bone folder to flatten the central crease.

For a woodland-themed party, or if you'd just love a touch of whimsy on your breakfast table, this place card is a simple project for a beginner papercutter.

Tool kit
- Bone folder
- Metal safeguard ruler
- Self-healing cutting mat
- Craft knife and blades

Materials
- Medium-weight cardstock
- Sticky tape

Choosing materials
You want your place card to stand up nicely when it is finished, so it's best to use a medium-weight cardstock of about 65 lb cover (176 gsm).

1 Cut out template 40 on page 127. To use the template more than once, print, copy, or transfer the template using one of the methods on page 16.

2 Take a piece of cardstock at least as wide and twice as tall as the template. Using a metal ruler and bone folder, fold the cardstock in half lengthwise. Scoring the line first will help you to create a nice, sharp crease.

3 Place the printed template on the cardstock with the fawn's ears and back flush against the folded edge. Tape the template in place. From here we have removed the template for clarity.

4 Using a craft knife on a cutting mat, first cut out the details on the fawn's face, working from his nose up to his ear. When cutting a long, curved shape such as the fawn's cheek, don't try to cut it all at once— lift up the blade every so often, reposition the paper to suit your arm movement, then continue cutting.

5 Cut out the spots along the fawn's back, working from right to left.

6 Using a metal ruler, cut a straight line across the bottom of the place card.

Template is on page 127

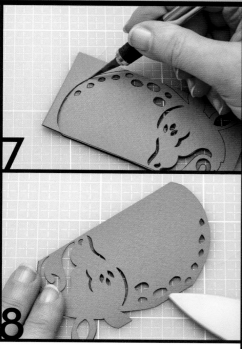

7 Finally, cut around the curve of the fawn's back and head to finish the template. Be careful around the small gap between the two ears.

8 Remove the template and reverse the fold so the cleaner-cut inside is now the outside. Use a bone folder to get a crisp, clean fold.

58 PLACE MAT

This lovely nature-inspired design will add something extra to your dinner-party table. Use the simple design or take it to another level by adding the extra details for a more advanced papercut.

Tool kit
- Bone folder
- Metal safeguard ruler
- Self-healing cutting mat
- Craft knife and blades

Materials
- Paper
- Sticky tape

Choosing materials
You can use any craft paper for this project—a weight of around 20 lb bond (75 gsm) would be about right—and Ledger size is perfect for a place mat.

1 Cut out template 39 on page 125. To use the template more than once, print, copy, or transfer the template using one of the methods on page 16.

2 Take a Ledger size piece of your chosen paper and fold in half widthways. Use a bone folder to make a sharp crease.

3 Place the printed template on the paper so decorated edge is flush against the open edge. Tape the template in place. From here we have removed the template for clarity.

4 Using a craft knife on a cutting mat, start by cutting out the squirrel at the bottom of the design. Start from his head then work through the details on his body before cutting the outline. Move onto the small leaves and the larger maple leaves.

5 Cut the details on the tree, beginning with the bark toward the bottom and moving up to the foliage. Cut out the side of the tree. Cut around the tiny squirrel on the side of the tree first, as this shape is the most important to cut accurately.

2

3

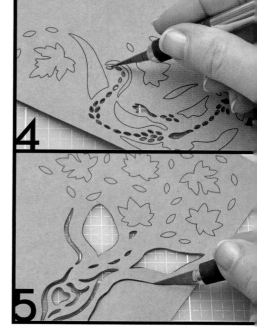

4

5

Advanced cuts

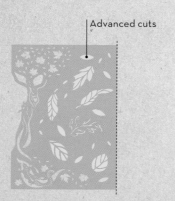

Template is on page 125

6 Finally, cut the leaves at the top of the tree. Start with the small leaves and move up to the larger maple leaves. If you're feeling adventurous, move onto Step 7, or skip straight to Step 8.

7 Cut some or all of the yellow-colored leaves in the center part of the design. Remember to begin with the smallest shapes and those closest to the fold line.

8 Remove the template and unfold the papercut. Use a bone folder to smooth down the central crease line. To make your place mats reusable and wipe-clean, why not take them down to a copy or office-supply store and have them laminated?

This design will add a whimsical air to your baby photo, whether for your own precious bundle or as a gift. The banner across the center allows you to personalize it further.

Tool kit
- Bone folder
- Metal safeguard ruler
- Self-healing cutting mat
- Craft knife and blades
- Craft screw punch

Materials
- Colored paper
- Medium-weight cardstock in a contrasting color
- Sticky tape
- Glue
- Double-sided tape

Choosing materials
I would recommend a heavy-weight paper of approximately 28 lb bond (105 gsm) for this project, as the papercut part of the frame does not need to stand alone, but you don't want it to be too flimsy. Try a heavier cardstock of around 110 lb cover (270 gsm) for the backing.

1 Cut out template 17 on page 103. To use the template more than once, print, copy, or transfer the template using one of the methods on page 16.

2 Take a piece of colored paper at least as tall as and twice the width of your template. Using a bone folder and metal ruler, fold the colored paper in half widthwise and tape the template onto the paper with the center of the design flush up against the folded edge. From here we have removed the template for clarity.

3 Using a craft knife and metal ruler on a cutting mat, start by cutting the straight edges in all the shapes along the border of the template.

4 Cut out the storks. Begin with the stork at the bottom, starting with his legs and working up to the wing tips. Now cut out the stork at the top. Use the screw punch to create eyes.

5 Cut out the clouds, working from the folded edge outward.

6 Cut the remainder of the shapes along the border of the frame.

Template is on page 103

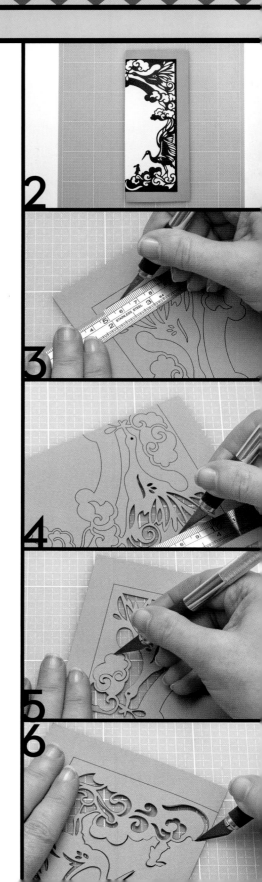

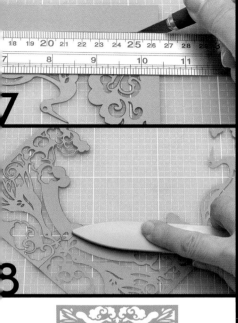

7 Using a craft knife and metal ruler on a cutting mat, carefully cut the outline of the frame.

8 Remove the template and unfold the paper. Use the bone folder to flatten the central crease.

9 Use double-sided tape to attach your chosen photograph to a piece of cardstock in a contrasting color that is larger than the frame. Tape or glue the frame to the background and trim the backing cardstock to size if needed.

Projects

Layering papercuts is a great way to add depth and interest to your artwork. Use different colors for each layer and create a beautiful scene.

Tool kit
- Bone folder
- Metal safeguard ruler
- Self-healing cutting mat
- Craft knife and blades

Materials
- Cardstock in four contrasting colors
- Sticky tape
- Double-sided tape
- Foam sticky dots (optional)

Choosing materials
Select colored cardstock for the four layers of your shadow box: the top, middle, bottom, and background. Choose colors that complement each other but are different enough that the layers remain distinct. Think about the order you want the colors to go in. The cardstock for the middle layer should be no more than 20 lb bond (75 gsm) as it will be folded twice. Approximately 80 lb text (120 gsm) is right for the other three layers.

| Top layer | Middle layer | Bottom layer |

Templates are on pages 129 and 131

1 Cut out three parts of template 43 on pages 129 and 131. To use the template more than once, print, copy, or transfer the template using one of the methods on page 16.

2 Take the cardstock for the top and bottom layers and, using a bone folder and metal ruler, fold each in half widthwise. Tape each template to the correct cardstock with the center of the design flush up against the folded edge.

3 Take the paper for the middle layer. Fold it in half twice to form a square. Use the bone folder to make the folds as smooth and flat as possible. Tape the middle template so that the top and left edges are flush with the folded edges of the square. From here we have removed the template for clarity.

4 Start with whichever layer you prefer. For each, using a craft knife on a cutting mat, begin with the smallest shapes. For the top layer this is the bear's eye, ear, and fur details. On the bottom layer, begin with the triangular trees. On the middle layer, start with the bark details and make sure you cut away from the center of the tree. This will prevent the paper from dragging and folding.

5 On the top layer, cut the grass. Cut from the root upward so the paper won't drag with the blade. On the bottom layer, cut the snow and the waves.

6 Cut all the remaining shapes from the border inward.

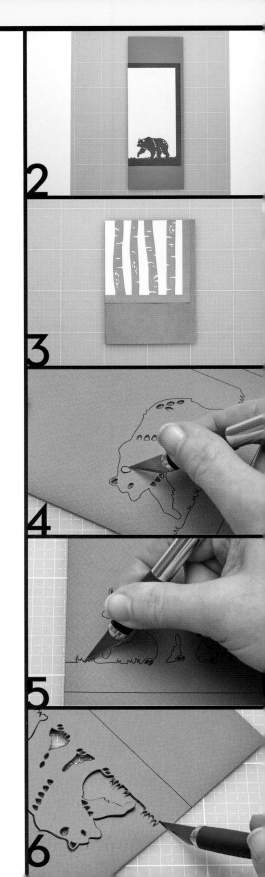

7 Using a craft knife and metal ruler on a cutting mat, carefully cut the outline of the frame on each layer.

8 Remove the templates and unfold the papers. Use the bone folder to flatten the central creases.

9 Use foam sticky dots or double-sided tape to stick the three layers together, being careful to precisely line up the edges for a neat finish.

10 Use double-sided tape to attach the papercut to the background cardstock. Trim the backing paper to size, and your shadow box is ready for framing.

This garland features simple cuts that make a big impact. Keep adding eggs in different colors until your garland is long enough.

Tool kit
- Bone folder
- Metal safeguard ruler
- Self-healing cutting mat
- Craft knife and blades
- Craft screw punch
- Scissors (optional)

Materials
- Colored paper
- Sticky tape
- Twine or ribbon
- Glue (optional)

Choosing materials
Choose a thin cardstock of around 80 lb text (120 gsm) instead of paper if you want your garland to be able to withstand being used more than once, although this will make cutting more difficult. Why not make motifs in all the colors of the rainbow?

1 Cut out template 25 on page 115. If you want to make a long garland, you might find it useful to have multiple copies of the template, so use one of the methods on page 16 to print or copy multiple templates. Alternatively, transfer the template to your chosen paper the desired number of times.

2 Take a piece of colored paper at least as tall and twice as wide as the template. Using a metal ruler and bone folder, fold the paper in half widthwise.

3 Place the printed template on the cardstock with the center of the egg flush against the folded edge. Tape the template in place. From here we have removed the template for clarity.

4 Use a screw punch to punch the circular shapes in the egg. The circle at the top of the egg is to thread the twine or ribbon through, and can be cut with a craft knife or punched.

5 Using a craft knife on a cutting mat, cut the petals on each flower. Start at the point of the petal nearest the fold line and move your blade outward.

Template is on page 115

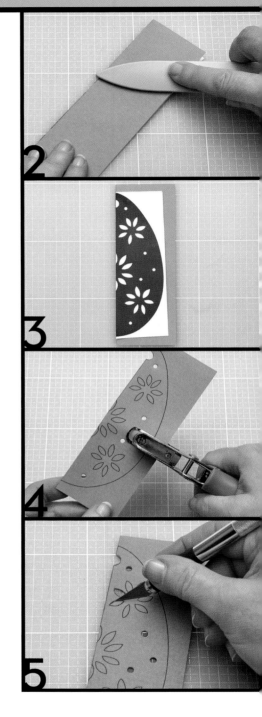

6 Cut around the outline of the egg. You could use scissors for this step instead of the craft knife, if you prefer.

7 Remove the template and unfold the papercut. Use the bone folder to flatten and smooth the central crease.

8 When you have the desired number of motifs, cut a length of twine or ribbon and thread it through the center-top hole of each egg motif, making sure they are evenly spaced. Either go around the top of the papercut and through each hole twice, or add a dab of glue to make sure that the motifs stay in place.

Projects

This simple silhouette design is the perfect project to get you familiar with the basics of papercutting. These easy-to-make toppers are the perfect addition to any party.

Tool kit
• Bone folder
• Metal safeguard ruler
• Self-healing cutting mat
• Craft knife and blades
• Scissors (optional)

Materials
• Cardstock
• Tooth picks
• Sticky tape
• Washi tape or glue

Choosing materials
You can use any weight of cardstock for this project—but stay away from anything too thick, as it will make cutting more difficult. Play around with different colors, or even try patterned paper for added detail.

Template is on page 117

1 Cut out template 29 on page 117. To use the template more than once, print, copy, or transfer the template using one of the methods on page 16.

2 Take a piece of the cardstock at least as tall and twice as wide as the template. Using a metal ruler and bone folder, fold the cardstock in half widthwise. Scoring the line first will help you to create a sharp crease.

3 Place the printed template on the cardstock with the center of the feather flush against the folded edge. Tape the template in place. From here we have removed the template for clarity.

4 Using a craft knife on a cutting mat, cut out all the inlets around the edge. Be sure to move your blade from the feather outward to avoid slipping or overcutting.

5 Cut around the outline of the feather. You could use a pair of scissors rather than your craft knife for this step, if you prefer.

6 Remove the template and unfold the papercut. Use a bone folder to flatten and smooth the central crease.

7 Use washi tape to secure the cake topper onto a tooth pick. Alternatively, make two feathers and glue together, sandwiching a tooth pick in the middle for a cake topper that looks flawless from both sides.

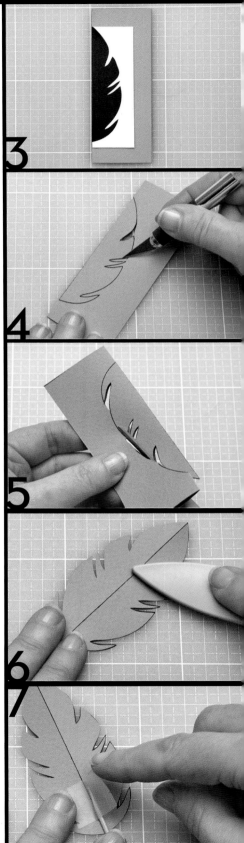

This 3D stag's head is a striking and modern decoration that really packs a punch. Match it to your color scheme and it's the perfect addition to your Christmas tree or holiday decorations.

Tool kit
- Bone folder
- Metal safeguard ruler
- Self-healing cutting mat
- Craft knife and blades
- Craft screw punch

Materials
- Medium-weight cardstock
- Ribbon

Choosing materials
To create a tree ornament that will retain its structure, and to make sure the antlers of your stag don't flop over, you should use a medium-weight cardstock of about 60–65 lb cover (160–176 gsm) for this project.

1 Turn to template 45 on page 137. You will need two copies of this template, so use one of the methods on page 16 to transfer two copies of the template onto the cardstock. Alternatively, photocopy the template or access using the QR code and print two copies onto regular printer paper, and tape to the cardstock. Whichever method you use, position the templates right of center on the cardstock.

2 Fold the cardstock in half widthwise with the printed template facing up. The edge of the template should align exactly along the center crease. To cleanly fold the cardstock, first lay the metal ruler in the correct place and use the bone folder to etch a sharp crease line—this will guide your fold. As you fold, apply even pressure with the bone folder to smooth down the crease and create a clean fold.

3 Use the screw punch to punch out the eyelet at the top of each antler.

4 Using a craft knife on a cutting mat, cut out all the details on the stag's face and the hollows in the antlers.

5 Cut the outline of the stag. Begin at the bottom of the face and work your way up, around the antlers, and finish at the top of the head.

6 Unfold the papercut and use a bone folder to smooth down the central crease. Repeat Steps 2–5 on the second stag. Unfold both.

Template is on page 137

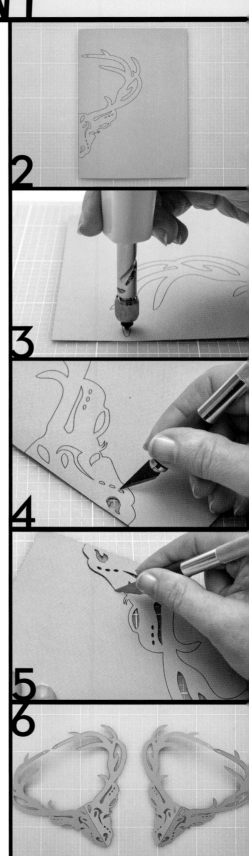

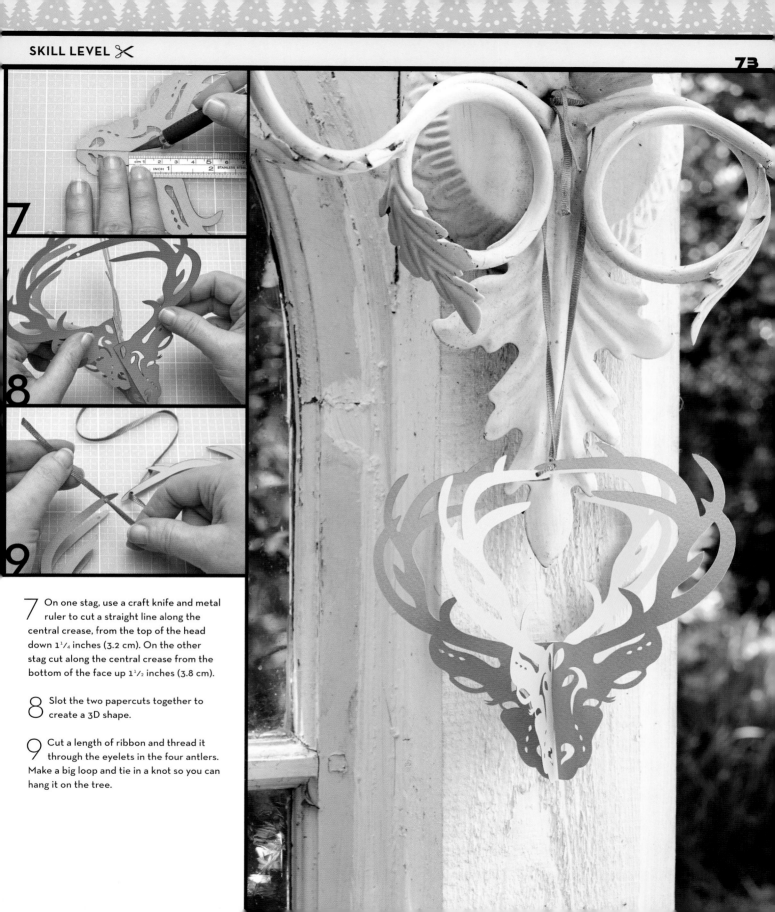

7 On one stag, use a craft knife and metal
ruler to cut a straight line along the
central crease, from the top of the head
down 1¼ inches (3.2 cm). On the other
stag cut along the central crease from the
bottom of the face up 1½ inches (3.8 cm).

8 Slot the two papercuts together to
create a 3D shape.

9 Cut a length of ribbon and thread it
through the eyelets in the four antlers.
Make a big loop and tie in a knot so you can
hang it on the tree.

LANTERN

This versatile project can be used as a tealight lantern, hung up as a garden decoration, or used as a favor box. It's a great example of how papercutting can personalize and elevate a simple DIY project.

Tool kit
- Bone folder
- Metal safeguard ruler
- Self-healing cutting mat
- Craft knife and blades
- Craft screw punch

Materials
- Medium-weight cardstock
- Rice, tissue, or vellum paper
- Sticky tape
- Twine
- Glue

Choosing materials
You want the lantern to stand up and maintain its structure, so a cardstock of about 60–65 lb cover (160–176 gsm) would be ideal. You could use a lighter-weight cardstock if the lantern is going to be purely decorative. Choose a light color for the tissue, rice, or vellum paper so lots of light can shine through like a stained-glass window.

Template is on page 119

1 Cut out template 35 on page 119. To use the template more than once, print, copy, or transfer the template using one of the methods on page 16.

2 Take a piece of your chosen cardstock that is at least as tall and twice as wide as the template. Using a metal ruler and bone folder, fold the paper in half widthwise. Scoring the line first will help you to create a sharp crease.

3 Place the printed template on the cardstock with the tab-free edge flush against the folded edge. Tape the template in place. From here we have removed the template for clarity.

4 Use a screw punch to create the two holes at the top of the template.

5 Using a craft knife on a cutting mat, first cut the ribbon-like details in the leaves.

6 Cut out the center petals in the large rose on the right-hand panel.

7 Using a metal ruler to help you, cut along all the straight edges.

8 Cut the remaining shapes on each panel. Start from the top and work your way downward.

9 Using a metal ruler, cut along the outside edge of the template.

10 Unfold the papercut. Use a bone folder and metal ruler to etch along all of the dotted fold lines, then remove the template.

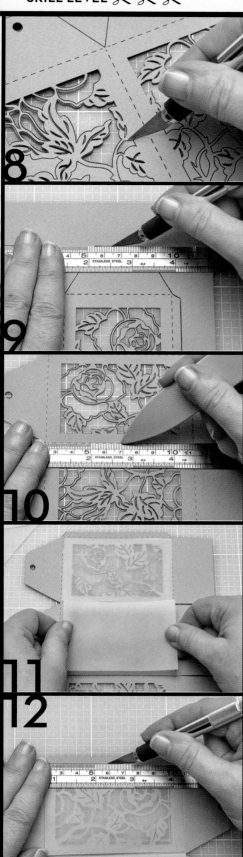

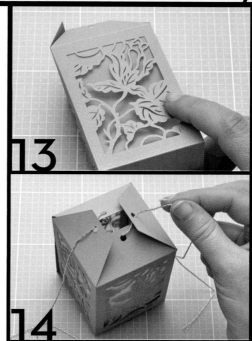

11 Take a sheet of rice, tissue, or vellum paper and cut out 2¼- x 3½-inch (6- x 9-cm) rectangles. Using a glue stick, attach one rectangle to each of the papercut panels.

12 Using the craft knife and metal ruler, cut off the slim tab on one end of the papercut only.

13 Flip the papercut over so the tissue paper is at the back. Fold along each of the etched lines to form a box shape, and use glue or tape on the side tab and the two bottom tabs to secure.

14 Place your tealight or party favors inside. Bring the top panels together and thread some twine through the holes and tie in a bow to close the lantern.

Safety first!
Only use battery-operated tealights with this project.

Mobiles are a staple in any child's room. This dream-catcher-style design gives you the freedom to make your papercut as intricate and as colorful as you like.

Tool kit
- Bone folder
- Metal safeguard ruler
- Self-healing cutting mat
- Craft knife and blades
- Hot glue gun
- Scissors

Materials
- Light-weight paper
- Sticky tape
- Twine
- Glue
- 6-inch (15-cm) embroidery hoop

Choosing materials
You will be cutting through seven layers of paper (including the template) to create the central web of the mobile, so I would recommend using a light-weight paper of no more than 20 lb bond (75 gsm). You could use the same for the butterflies for a delicate look, or use a slightly heavier-weight cardstock if you prefer.

Template is on page 117

1 Cut out four parts of template 34 on page 117. To use the template more than once, print, copy, or transfer the template using one of the methods on page 16.

2 To create the sun fold (see page 14), take a square piece of your chosen paper and use a metal ruler and bone folder to etch down the middle of the paper, horizontally and vertically. Then etch the two diagonal lines, corner to corner, through the center point. Using these creases as a guide, fold the paper into a triangular shape.

3 Place the printed template on the paper so the lines of the web are flush against the folded edges of the triangle and the point is right in the corner. Tape the template in place. From here we have removed the template for clarity.

4 Using a craft knife on a cutting mat, carefully cut out the web design. Remove the template and unfold the papercut. Use a bone folder to flatten and smooth the creases.

5 Position the paper web in the bottom part of the embroidery hoop. You don't need any glue at this point as you will tighten the frame around the hoop to secure it in place. However, you could add a few spots of glue if you like.

6 Place the top part of the embroidery hoop on top, and tighten.

7 Take a piece of the paper you have chosen for the butterflies, at least as tall and twice as wide as the templates. Using a metal ruler and bone folder, fold the paper in half widthwise. Etching the line first will help you to create a sharp crease.

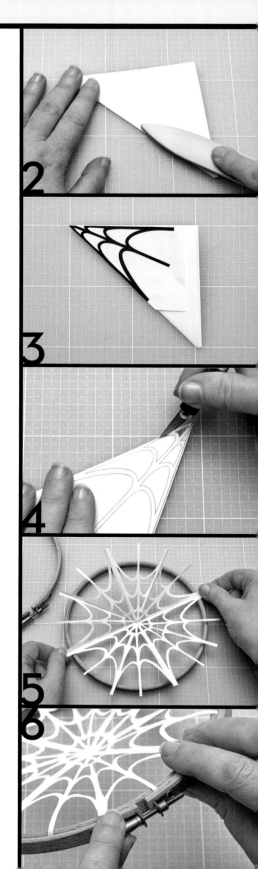

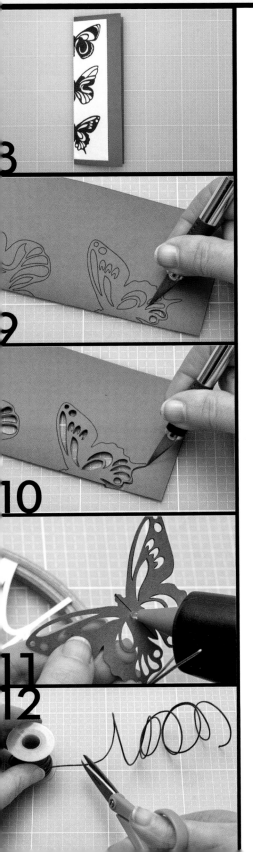

8 Place the printed template on the cardstock with the center of the butterflies' bodies flush against the folded edge. Tape the template in place. We have provided three butterfly templates here. I would recommend photocopying or printing this template three times so you can create nine butterflies in total for a beautiful mobile. You could pick three colored papers and make three butterflies in each color. From here we have removed the template for clarity.

9 Cut the internal details on the wings of each butterfly. Begin with the cuts closest to the folded edge and work your way outward.

10 Carefully cut around the edge of each butterfly. Remove the templates and unfold the papercuts. Use a bone folder to smooth out the central crease.

11 Use a hot glue gun to attach one butterfly to the center-top of the web.

12 Cut three lengths of twine roughly 12 inches (30 cm) in length.

13 Add a dab of glue to the back of each butterfly and attach to the twine. Divide them between the lengths of twine, and space them out.

14 You could cut out double the number of butterflies and stick them together with the twine sandwiched in the middle to make butterflies that look good from every angle.

15 Glue the lengths of twine to the bottom of the embroidery hoop. Attach a length of twine to the top of the hoop for hanging, and leave the glue to dry thoroughly.

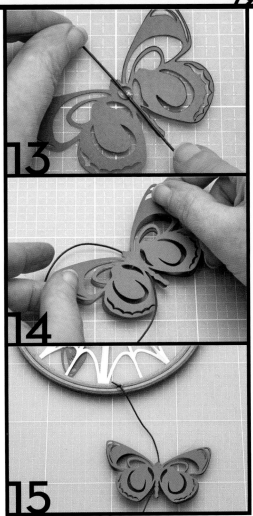

As you saw in the Crown project on pages 42–43, you can use a half-image and an accordion fold to create a repeating pattern of a whole image. This technique could be replicated using any of the other mirror-fold projects in the book to make a paperchain for any occasion.

Tool kit
• Bone folder
• Metal safeguard ruler
• Self-healing cutting mat
• Craft knife and blades

Materials
• Paper
• Sticky tape

Choosing materials
There are many folds in this project, so you will want to use a light-weight paper. I would recommend sticking to 16–20 lb bond (60–75 gsm).

1 Turn to template 47 on page 141. Measure the width of the template and then mark this point on your chosen paper. Using this mark as your guide, fold your chosen paper accordion style (see page 13) as many times as desired. I would recommend cutting through a maximum of eight layers of paper at a time.

2 Use one of the methods on page 16 to transfer the template to your chosen paper. This way you will not have any extra layers or templates to contend with. Alternatively, photocopy the template or access using the QR code and print onto regular printer paper, and tape to the paper. Whichever method you use, position the template so it lies flush against both edges of the paper. From here we have removed the template for clarity.

3 Using a craft knife on a cutting mat, start by cutting the pumpkin's eyes and mouth.

4 Cut the pumpkin's stem. Start from the top with the semicircle on the fold line and work outward and downward.

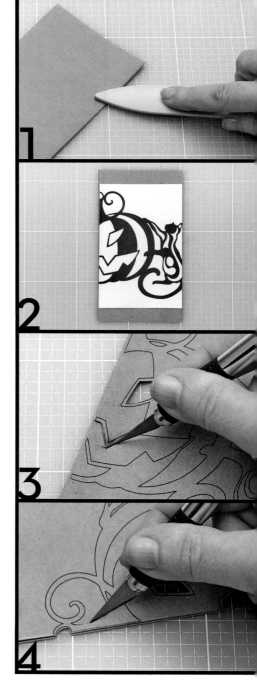

Template is on page 141

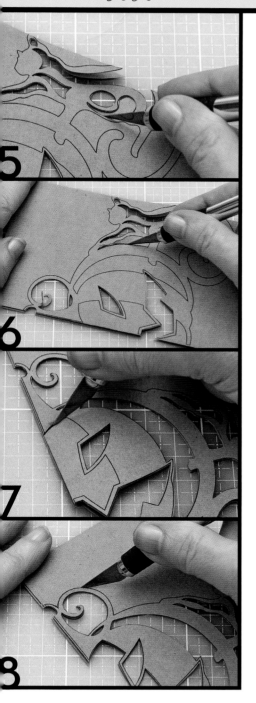

5 Leave the rest of the pumpkin uncut and move onto the cat. Cut out all the inside shapes of the cat's silhouette.

6 Cut out the hollows between the cat and the pumpkin. When cutting along the cat's tail, move the paper around as you cut to better follow the line.

7 Cut the two stripes on the pumpkin. Start with the one closest to the cat.

8 Now cut carefully around the outline of the papercut.

9 Unfold the papercut chain to reveal the design. Use clear sticky tape to connect multiple chains together to create one long chain that can go around the room.

This project will show you how to cut your very own floral cake topper to cheer up all types of cakes and occasions. With room to write a personal salutation, your options are endless!

Tool kit
- Bone folder
- Metal safeguard ruler
- Self-healing cutting mat
- Craft knife and blades

Materials
- Medium-weight cardstock
- Sticky tape
- Washi tape
- Bamboo skewers

Choosing materials
You want your cake topper to stand up proud on the cake and not flop over, so it's best to use a medium-weight cardstock of about 60–65 lb cover (160–176 gsm) for this project.

1 Cut out template 46 on page 139. To use the template more than once, print, copy, or transfer the template using one of the methods on page 16.

2 Take a piece of the cardstock for the cake topper—it should be at least as tall and twice as wide as the template. Using a metal ruler and bone folder, fold the cardstock in half widthwise. Etching the line first will help you to create a sharp crease.

3 Place the printed template on the cardstock with the center of the design flush against the folded edge. Tape the template in place. From here we have removed the template for clarity.

4 Using a craft knife on a cutting mat, cut the details inside the ribbon, and the small pollen shapes inside the centers of the flowers.

5 Cut out the hollows between the flowers and the ribbon.

6 Now cut out the petals on all of the flowers, and the leaves.

7 This is the hardest part. Cut around the outline of the papercut. Start with the outline farthest from the fold, and move inward. Hold down the paper as you go to prevent it from shifting.

8 Carefully unfold the papercut to reveal the design. Use the bone folder to smooth down the central crease, and write your message on the front of the banner.

9 Using washi tape, attach two bamboo skewers to the back of the papercut and place it on top of your cake.

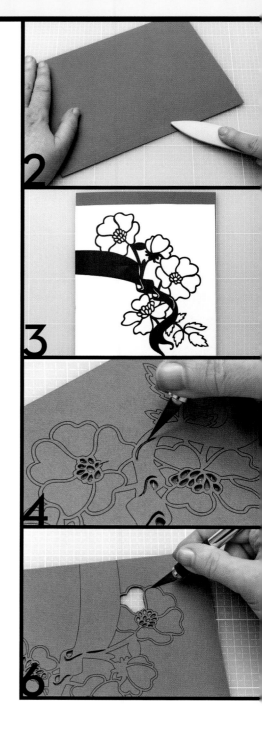

Template is on page 139

2

TEMPLATES

In this chapter you will find the templates for 48 beautiful and unique papercutting projects. Every template is numbered, so you can easily find the right template for the project you are working on. There are also "variation" templates for many of the projects, and some bonus templates that aren't linked to one specific project but are there for you to experiment with your newfound papercutting skills.

A dotted line is marked down the inside edge of each page to show you where you could cut if you want to use the templates straight out of the book. Use a metal safeguard ruler, self-healing cutting mat, and craft knife to do this. Many of the pages have more than one template, so you might want to use a pair of scissors to cut out the individual templates as you need them, rather than removing the whole page.

If you don't want to cut up the book then you don't have to! You can scan the QR code on page 144 to access all of the templates on your computer, and then print them onto regular printer paper as many times as you like to use again and again. You can also trace or photocopy the templates so you can resize or modify them. Or use one of the methods on page 16 to transfer the template straight onto your chosen papercutting paper—so you won't need to attach a template at all.

Get cutting and have fun!

TEMPLATE 1
**Kissing
Squirrels Card,
pages 20–21**

TEMPLATE 2
My Deer Card,
pages 24–25

TEMPLATE 3
Fairy Ring Card,
pages 54–55

TEMPLATE 4
**Enchanted
Castle Card,
pages 46–47**

TEMPLATE 5
Leafy Gift Wrap, pages 32–33

TEMPLATE 7
**Leafy Ribbon,
pages 40–41**

TEMPLATE 6
**Leafy Gift Tag,
pages 26–27**

TEMPLATES 8–10
Use with a mirror fold, page 12

TEMPLATES 11–12
Use with a mirror fold, page 12

TEMPLATES 14–15
Wedding Invitation variations, pages 30–31

TEMPLATE 13
Wedding Invitation, pages 30–31

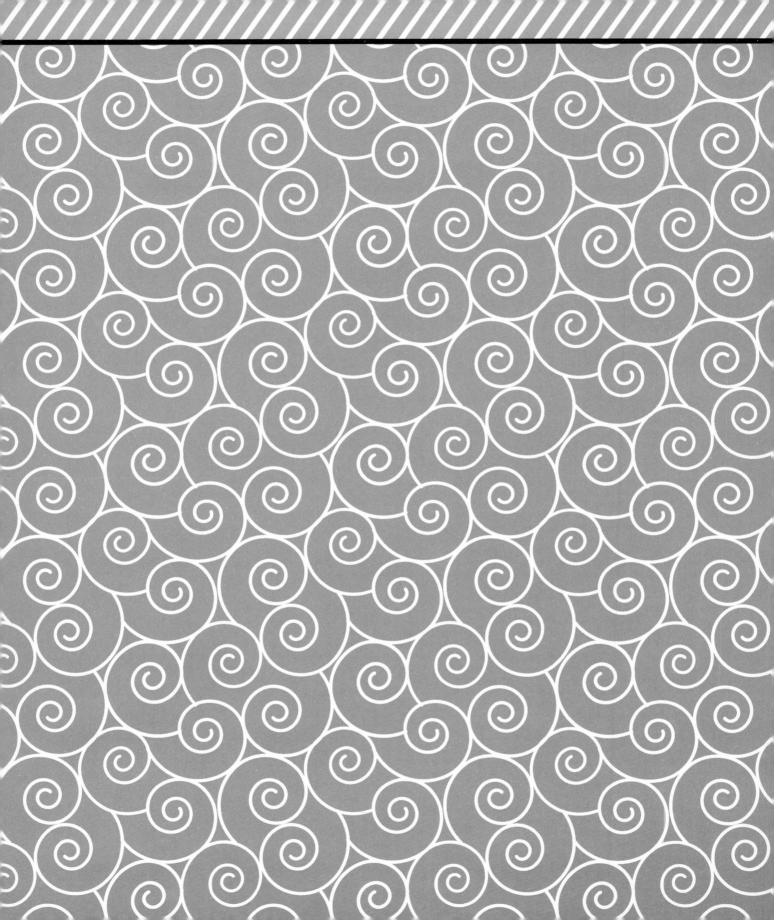

TEMPLATE 16
**Flower
Arrangement,
pages 52–53**

TEMPLATE 17
**Baby Photo
Frame,
pages 62–63**

TEMPLATE 18
**Feather Crown,
pages 42–43**

TEMPLATE 19
**Crown variation,
pages 42–43**

TEMPLATE 20
Use with a mirror fold, page 12

TEMPLATE 21
Use with a quarter fold, page 13

TEMPLATE 22
**Swan Necklace,
pages 34–35**

TEMPLATE 23
Fox Mask,
pages 36–37

TEMPLATE 24
Family Tree,
pages 48–49

TEMPLATE 25
Easter Garland,
pages 68–69

TEMPLATES 26–27
Easter Garland
variations,
pages 68–69

TEMPLATE 28
Use with a
quarter fold,
page 13

TEMPLATE 29
**Feather
Cupcake
Topper,
pages 70–71**

TEMPLATES 30–33
**Feather Cupcake
Topper variations,
pages 70–71**

TEMPLATE 34
**Mobile,
pages 78–79**

TEMPLATE 35
**Lantern,
pages 74–75**

TEMPLATE 36
Lantern variation, pages 74–75

TEMPLATE 37
**Use with a
mirror fold,
page 12**

TEMPLATE 38
**Cake Topper
variation,
pages 84–85**

TEMPLATE 39
Place Mat,
pages 58–59.

Yellow areas
are optional,
advanced cuts.

TEMPLATE 40
**Fawn Place Card,
pages 56–57**

TEMPLATE 41
**Place Card
variation,
pages 56–57**

TEMPLATE 42
**Place Card
variation,
pages 56–57**

TEMPLATE 43
Shadow Box
(top and middle
layers),
pages 64-65

TEMPLATE 43
**Shadow Box
(bottom layer),
pages 64–65**

TEMPLATE 44
**Shadow Box
variation
(top layer),
pages 64–65**

TEMPLATE 44
**Shadow Box
variation
(bottom layer),
pages 64-65**

TEMPLATE 44
**Shadow Box
variation
(middle layer),
pages 64–65**

TEMPLATE 45
**Stag Tree
Ornament,
pages 73–74**

TEMPLATE 46
**Cake Topper,
pages 84–85**

TEMPLATE 47
**Halloween
Paperchain,
pages 80–81**

TEMPLATE 48
**Paperchain
variation,
pages 80–81**

CREDITS

Author acknowledgments
My sincerest thanks to the team at Quarto for taking a chance on me and elevating my papercuts—the book would not exist without you! A special thanks to Susan Niner Janes whose hands appear in the demonstrations in this book where mine could not.

To Ayelet Sapir and Tali Yalonetzki who first encouraged me to turn to papercutting, your kind words were the seed of all that came after; I would not be doing this without your praise and encouragement—and for that I am forever grateful.

The book is dedicated to my mom and sister, who put up with me throughout the creation of this book. Your feedback and your faith in me were—and are always—invaluable!

Publisher credits

Get the templates

 Use the QR code or the URL to access the templates.

www.quartoknows.com/
page/fold-it